RELATING

Reflections
of a
Psychologist

RELATING

Reflections
of a
Psychologist

Alan G. Rauchway, Ph.D.

AVERY PUBLISHING GROUP INC.
Wayne, New Jersey

Front cover art: From *Three Spheres II* by M. C. Escher.
Reprinted by permission of the Escher Foundation —
  Haags Gemeentemuseum — The Hague.

ISBN 0-89529-290-4

Printed in the United States of America

10 9 8 7 6 5 4 3 2 1

**Dedicated
to
my wife
Dale
and my children
Drew Barry
and
Marisa Ann**

Acknowledgements

I would like to thank the following people who were very helpful to me in the writing of this book: my wife, Dale, my dear friend, Eleanore Lubin, and my good friends, Jeanette Delponte and Laura Wadenpfuhl. They were invaluable in the preparation and editing of this manuscript.

I would also like to thank my mother, Diane, and my sister, Ellen, for their support and helpful comments. In addition, Vita Tauss, Jerry Link, Shelly Goldstein, Mirta G. Marten, and Mary Ann Gittens, all made significant contributions in the evolution of this work.

Foreword

Relating to one's self and others in a constructive manner is vital to human development and survival. Our most basic psychological need is to feel worthy and acceptable to ourselves and others, "to love and to be loved." Yet, how are these universal needs valued in our society, and how are these needs taught? If I were totally alien to this society, what would I think of this society, in the way that people relate to one another, and to the way people treat one another? I would see this as a society of acquisition and competition, of power and dominance. Intimacy and cooperation, and therefore relating are sacrificed under the name of individual self-fulfillment.

The importance of relating has, in essence, and in effect, been denied. What I like most about this book, and what I feel most beneficial to you, the reader, is Dr. Rauchway's emphasis on mutual nurturance and understanding as a prime responsibility to all parties of a relationship. This is in contrast to all too common one-sidedness in a relationship whether that relationship be personal or professional. The valuable insights contained in this book function as a catalyst to educate, challenge, and stimulate the reader. I am certain that you, the reader, will see yourself in many of the life experiences or situations presented in this work. Hopefully, it can make a significant difference.

Dr. Eleanore Lubin
Practicing Psychoanalyst
New York City

Preface

As we grow older, we all experience the emotional pain that is a result of the death of loved ones and friends. This pain is unavoidable. However, there is a tremendous amount of pain and hurt that is the result of individuals not understanding themselves psychologically and not possessing the relating skills to carry on satisfying interpersonal relationships.

It is the purpose of this book to begin to rectify these deficiencies by presenting an abundance of concepts on psychological self-awareness, and on understanding the pitfalls and nuances involved in interpersonal relationships, as well as presenting many ideas dealing with effective relating.

Relating: Reflections of a Psychologist consists of over 250 disparate concepts presented in a clear, concise form so as to enhance understanding, and to stimulate thinking, as well as interest in the various topics. It is the product of my years of working as a clinical psychologist, college professor, and also the result of my own emotional and social development as a son, brother, husband, and father. I believe the serious reader can get a substantial "education" as well as have much to consider and discuss as he delves through this book. In any case, I hope the reader enjoys reading this work as much as I enjoyed writing it.

RELATING

In life, people owe us nothing except *decency*. Anything they give beyond this is special and should be *appreciated*. It is this capacity for appreciation of another person and his efforts which is a *major* distinguishing feature of being emotionally mature.

Emotionally mature people are *open* to *all* their feelings, fantasies, and thoughts. They do not judge or condemn any of these aspects of their "inner world." They are well aware that *all* feelings, fantasies, and thoughts are simply *human*, and as such, need simply to be *accepted* by the individual experiencing them. In essence, a person's "inner world" can *only* hurt this individual if he does not accept it, or tries to divide feelings into being either "good" or "bad."

Isn't it sad that society teaches individuals to dislike or even hate themselves for what they are experiencing in their "inner world." In reality, being a "good" or "bad" person depends solely on one's *words* and *actions* in relating to others. My thoughts, feelings, and fantasies cannot hurt another person if I simply keep them to myself.

It is an interesting point that while emotionally mature individuals are the most *open* to their feelings, fantasies and thoughts, they are also generally the most *sensitive* in discriminating which of these they will share with others, and which they will simply keep within themselves. In essence, caring is often shown more by what we do *not* share with another from one's "inner world" than by what we do share.

Many of our feelings are largely "selfish." This is not surprising as our feelings reflect our underlying needs. If I feel hungry, I am aware that I have a need to eat, etc. As such, these "selfish" feelings have biological and adaptive value. Just because I have "selfish" feelings does *not* make me a selfish person. Only my actions and words can do so.

How many times do people say to one another, "You should not feel that way" or "Why are you feeling that?" These people do not understand, like so many of us, that our feelings are largely spontaneous and uncontrollable, and as such, we have *no real say* in how we are going to feel. We are largely what we are feeling at any given moment, and to "put down" another human being for what he is feeling only serves to alienate and "turn off" the individual. In essence, I feel what I feel, and if you care about, and respect me, you are going to *accept* the feelings that I am sharing with you.

Fantasies (i.e. — daydreaming) can be a wonderful and satisfying inner experience. In our fantasies we can experience, through our imagination, all kinds of things without having to structure our fantasies to fit into a civilized or socially approved form. For example, we can have fantasies of a sexual or aggressive nature which society would never accept as "normal behavior." As long as we can separate our fantasies from reality, do not live in our fantasies to escape life, and are able to effectively decide which fantasies we will act on, and do not act on those which would result in antisocial behavior, then our fantasy life can be an effective "safety valve" to prevent antisocial behavior as well as *enriching* our lives.

There is *no* such thing as "love at first sight." How can you love another person without getting to know the person as a human being? What people call "love at first sight" is more accurately "lust at first sight!"

It is very important for parents to raise their children to be emotionally and financially *independent*. I have witnessed individuals take all types of emotional and/or physical abuse due to being dependent on another person in either or both of these areas.

Many of us do not relate effectively with ourselves or other people. In part this is due to our not understanding the distinction between our thinking and feeling processes. Unlike feelings, our thought processes are based more on logic and rationality (in the case of emotionally mature people), and to some extent, they can be controlled voluntarily. Our thinking processes can understand another person's motivations as well as circumstances (i.e. — I was two hours late for an appointment because my car broke down). On the other hand, as previously mentioned, our feelings are largely "selfish," self-centered, and revolve around our own needs. Thus, I can intellectually understand that you were two hours late because your car broke down, but I can still be angry because you did not meet my need, albeit unintentional.

At any moment in time, an individual is receiving imput from his feelings, as well as from his thinking processes. Psychological problems can arise when the person "tunes out" either of these imputs. The obsessive personality has largely lost touch with his feeling messages, while the person who is too into his feelings and impulses does not pay enough attention to his thinking processes.

Our society helps to create *all kinds* of psychological problems in its citizens by not presenting a *realistic, accurate* picture of what it means to be a *human being*.

6

When the caretakers in our lives, such as parents, teachers', etc. present a distorted picture of what it means to be a human being, the result is a continuous battle between the "real" human being that is within each of us, and the distorted illusion of ourselves that we try to copy—the result?—inner turmoil and feelings of great dislike and worthlessness.

Our society has been particularly negligent when it comes to educating its members about the nature and expression of our sexual and aggressive drives and desires.

If a parent wants a rough guideline to evaluate how a child's self-image (how the child feels about himself/herself) is developing, the parent can count the number of *realistically* complimentary things one says to this child as compared to the number of critical or abusive comments made during a typical day.

Many of us feel very uncomfortable when we feel angry, let alone expressing that anger. We are not born feeling this way: we are *taught* these feelings. How many times have we been criticized for feeling angry, when anger is simply a feeling, just as *valuable* and acceptable as *any* of our other feelings? It is the responsibility of every parent to teach his child that feeling angry is *human*, and to deny or "block out" one's inner experience of anger is dehumanizing, counterproductive, and can lead to significant psychological and physical difficulties.

I have met an enormous number of individuals who have never been taught to *express* their angry feelings in a *constructive* manner. Their resulting *destructive* expression of their angry feelings is not motivated by an attempt to resolve any conflicts so as to bring them closer to another person. Rather, they are trying to hurt, and to wound their perceived antagonist. In doing so, they may seriously damage their relationship. Calling another person abusive names (i.e. – dummy, fool, stupid, imbecile) communicates *no* useful information other than to perhaps damage another human being's self-image.

It is a wonderful feeling to know that your mate will be *open, honest*, and *constructive* in expressing his anger. This type of behavior on the part of both parties will significantly contribute to a relaxed relating atmosphere.

Emotionally mature individuals, when they are feeling angry in relating to another individual, are aware that they are usually *not* angry at that person. Rather, the angry individual is responding emotionally to another person's words, actions, lack of verbal response, and/or lack of actions. In essence, the response is to the individual's *behavior*. Only *repeated* or extreme perceived antagonistic behavior (in most cases) will evoke angry feelings toward the person, himself. In typical situations, therefore, the emotionally mature individual will express his anger in a *constructive* manner by sharing his thoughts and feelings *in order to bring himself closer to the other person*. Specifically, emotionally mature individuals will clearly state that they are feeling angry; try to explain what behavior evoked this angry response; and explain what would help correct the situation.

I have seen time after time in my psychotherapy practice where tremendous damage has been done in a relationship when one or both members are not aware when they are feeling angry at their mate's behavior. Even when they are aware, they often do not express it verbally, or if they do, they are destructive in the expression of their anger. The resulting increased animosity and distancing between the two people can, over time, damage what was once a caring relationship.

If I want to change your feelings (i.e. — you are feeling angry at my behavior), the best way is to:

1. Ask you to explain to me, as best you can, why you think you are feeling this way.

2. Tell you I will not interrupt, and I will give you my undivided attention until you are finished.

3. Fully accept how you are feeling, and tell you I do fully accept whatever you are feeling (i.e. — feeling angry). This may be the most important step of all.

4. Ask you to allow me the same courtesy I just gave you. Namely, to listen to me explain, as best as I can, my motivation or motivations for behaving the way I did, as I appeal to your thinking processes, namely the rational part of your personality, which *can* understand motivations and circumstances.

I have witnessed many "loving" individuals do some of the cruelest, most insensitive acts. In almost all cases this behavior was "triggered off" by this person feeling as if his *self-esteem* had been seriously wounded by another individual or group of individuals.

When an individual's emotional state is too intense (i.e. — *very* angry), it is difficult, if not impossible, to express accurately what he wishes to express to another person. In these instances, out of caring and respect for himself, the other person and the integrity of the relationship, it is imperative that he tell the person that he is too angry to accurately communicate at the moment. The individual should ask for time to collect his thoughts and feelings, and after he has done so, be prepared to sit down and communicate with the other person.

If a person you are relating to genuinely appears not to care that he is hurting you, then it is time to seriously consider saying "good-bye."

It is ironic that if you ask most people what they would like for themselves and their loved ones, many would state "happiness." Yet, how much time do people spend working on understanding their emotions, and how much effort did our parents put into their children's emotional and social development? Why is this? It is because our parents' emotional and social development was largely unintentionally neglected by *their* parents. Thus, it is not surprising that the major function of psychotherapy is the emotional and social re-education of the client.

Some individuals, when they are upset, need to be left alone. If you are relating to such an individual, the only thing you can do is to ask him whether it has anything to do with you, and if you can help him in any way. If he replies that he simply needs to be alone for a while, then it is important for the relationship that you respect this person's wishes. (P.S. – in these situations, if possible, the individual who wishes to be left alone should state whether he feels he will require a short amount of time, such as an hour, or a long amount of time. What is most important here, is that the person who wishes to be left alone, clearly indicate that he *will* relate to the other person in due time.)

Never try to analyze why you are feeling happy – simply *enjoy* it.

No matter how much you care about another person, there *will* be times when you cannot meet this person's needs. If this does happen occasionally, it in no way means that the relationship is a poor one. Each person, in any relationship, is ultimately responsible for taking care of himself.

If an individual wants to maximize his chances for inner peace, and to really enjoy relationships with others, then this person's development must include a clear understanding of one's "inner world." However, *this is not enough*. The individual must also develop a solid foundation in what constitutes *effective relating skills*. This education is a primary responsibility of society and its caretakers (i.e. — parents).

The quality of any relationship is defined by how well each individual perceives his needs are being met.

Having an effective relationship involves *hard work* as well as *courage* on the part of both members.

When an individual is upset over some aspect of a relationship, it is this person's responsibility and even *duty* to sit down and discuss it with the other individual. In essence, emotional cowardice is a major reason for the destruction of a relationship.

In many instances, there appears to be a close relationship between irrational guilt feelings on the one hand, and selfishness and manipulative behavior on the other. This often stems from the way we were raised. If one or both parents have selfish, unrealistic expectations of us, and we either do not or cannot meet their implicit or explicit demands, or we meet them even though, on a feeling level, we do *not* want to do so, then marked, irrational guilt feelings may result. When the same individual later experiences these guilt feelings at various times during his lifetime, then he needs to ask himself whether the individual or individuals he is relating to are once again exhibiting selfish, manipulative, exploitative behavior. At the core of this maladaptive interaction is the implied or explicit message that the individual is causing grave emotional damage by not giving into the selfish demands of the parents and/or peers.

In order to experience effective, emotionally satisfying relationships, an individual must be able to take an honest look at his motivations and behavior, and if warranted, be able to genuinely say "I am sorry." This is crucial to keeping the relationships alive and well.

If you are having a disagreement with someone, and you genuinely believe that the person's emotional reaction is too intense for what is apparently bothering the other person, then this "overreaction" may be a "tip off" that something else is actually at the core of this emotional response. *Gently* pointing this out to the person *may*, in some instances, evoke what is especially bothering the person.

If you continue to argue with someone over something that does not appear to be reaching any sort of constructive resolutions, then it is often beneficial to ask the following two questions of yourself and of the other person:

1. What is the underlying theme of what you are telling me?

2. Is there any basic human need that you feel I am violating?

If you are unable to determine why your relationship appears to not be working, informally count how many genuinely caring, positive statements are made when you are relating with the other individual as opposed to the number of critical, negative, denigrating type of statements.

If you want your mate to become more affectionate, attentive, animated, etc., then it is time for *you* to initiate being more affectionate, attentive, animated, etc.

Every individual needs to have an activity or activities which he enjoys or gives him satisfaction outside of his relationship. This will actually improve the quality of the relationship as both people will have more "emotional energy" to share with one another.

I believe that each of us is born with an emotional "love vat," which contains emotional energy for living. I also believe that these emotional energies can be replenished as well as depleted in our daily living.

There are certain individuals who are emotionally replenishing to be with; others who are emotionally depleting. Emotionally mature individuals try to spend as much time as is reasonable with the emotional replenishers.

It is an interesting point, that generally when two emotionally mature people are relating *each* will feel somewhat emotionally replenished being in the company of the other person.

There are certain *activities* that people find emotionally replenishing (i.e. — enjoying listening to music), others they deem to be emotionally debilitating (i.e. — studying very boring material); and there are still other activities which are neither emotionally enhancing nor emotionally draining (watching a mildly interesting T.V. show).

The *best* sexual foreplay is what is done *out* of the bedroom (i.e. — the quality of the verbal communication, the quality and quantity of considerate acts towards one another, the degree of emotional rapport, etc.). It is amazing and disillusioning how little time is spent emotionally relating in this manner, and thus, it is not surprising how many couples feel dissatisfied relating sexually *in* the bedroom.

Many parents have a lot of anxiety when handling sibling rivalry (jealousy and competition between children). I have heard a number complain how one of their children talks about "hating" a brother or sister. In actuality, it is much better for the child to talk about his negative feelings, as opposed to using *action*, such as hitting a sibling, or totally inhibiting these feelings and thoughts, which emotionally constricts the child, hindering his spontaneity.

I have treated a number of individuals who had a great need to be "perfect." In all cases, there existed a self-hating (masochistic), "unaccepting-of-oneself" component in each of these individuals' personalities. This type of problem typically reflects having experienced a very critical, emotionally abusive upbringing. The individual, therefore, tries to make himself "invulnerable" by being "perfect" so as not to be criticized, or "put down" again. If the therapy was successful, this need for perfection was replaced by a desire simply to be "human."

If an individual experiences unhappy relationships with one or both parents early in his life, then he may unconsciously seek out individuals who are similar to his parent or parents. He tries to get this individual to love him so as to convince himself that his parents loved him also. This almost always leads to disastrous consequences, partly because the new individual, like the parent or parents, is too emotionally damaged to be loving to *anyone*.

Emotionally mature people do not try to put themselves in a superior position to others, nor in an inferior (or subservient) position. In essence, they do not try to emotionally distance themselves from others through either of these tactics. They simply want to be on an equal level. In doing so, they maximize their chances for emotionally intimate and satisfying relating.

One of the best ways to help your child (and anybody else) feel intrinsically loveable is to give them a hug and/or kiss just because you feel like it. It is a sad commentary that so many of us say "What do you want?", "What did I do?", or "What's wrong?", all suggesting that these individuals do not feel intrinsically loveable. In essence, they do not feel deserving of love simply for just being themselves. Why is this? This is because their parents only gave them love when they either performed up to their level of expectation, or when they simply conformed to their parents' wishes. How many of us, when we are spontaneously hugged and/or kissed simply respond by saying, "Thank you" or "I enjoyed that," suggesting we feel deserving of such loving behavior.

Wouldn't it be lovely to give gifts to loved ones and friends without there having to be a formal occasion (e.g. — birthday, Chanukah, Christmas). This is a sensitive and wonderful demonstration of caring.

There really is little or no relationship between the intellectual or academic development of an individual, and the person's growth in the areas of sensitivity, emotional functioning, and social development. Therefore, it is not surprising that some of our brightest individuals (e.g. — college professors, doctors, scientists, lawyers, etc.) may be at much less advanced levels in these other realms. They may have invested so much energy and time in developing their intellects that these other realms of functioning have been grievously neglected; hence, the uneven development.

In order to have an effective relationship with another person, both parties must have the ability, and utilize the capacity to be a *good* listener, so as to *clearly* understand the needs of the other person. How many times have you tried to communicate your needs to someone else, and found that the latter was *only* interested in making his own points? This person puts little or no effort into listening to what you are trying to say.

There are times when your mate simply needs you *to be there;* *not* to judge or advise, but simply to be there, and be emotionally supportive.

When your mate is very upset, sometimes a reassuring *hug* is the *perfect* solution.

Effective relaters are aware that nonverbal cues, such as a squeeze on the arm, or a pat on the back, can be more reassuring and meaningful than a person's words.

It is perfectly acceptable that two individuals can have a loving relationship, yet have some interests or values that differ. The key is mutual *acceptance* and *respect* for the other person's different interests and/or values.

If an individual has developed normally, by the end of his adolescent years, he has become his own person, emotionally independent of his parents. (P.S. — this has *nothing*, and I *mean* nothing to do with loving or not loving them.)

When children grow up to be adults, themselves, their relationship is ideally that of *good friends* with their parents.

From the moment we join our mother and father at birth, it is the *great* task of parenting to prepare us more and more to go out into the world as self-caring, competent, and emotionally independent human beings. In essence, it is the *ultimate* loving act for parents to educate their children so they may someday leave them for a life of their own.

A significant number of parents actually believe (often based on the way *they* were raised), that their children will "pay us back" when they grow up. This is a selfish, unloving, callous position, which implies that parents have no obligations to their children in the process of raising them, and also that the children do not "give" a lot to *receptive* parents.

It is a sad commentary that so many marriages are seriously stressed or end in ruin. Very often it's not because both people cannot get along, but rather that one or both individuals are not emotionally independent of their respective families. As a result, they may not put their mate as number one, resulting in all sorts of animosities, hurts, and feelings of rejection.

The *best* indicator of how someone feels toward us is how this individual *treats* us.

If I were allowed to ask a couple only one question in order to help ascertain how good their relationship is, I would ask each of them, "Who is your best friend?"

One person *cannot* make another person "happy" for any length of time. One must be basically happy with oneself and one's life in order to be considered a "happy person." It is also an unfair as well as an unrealistic burden to place on another human being.

If you care about someone, that does *not* mean that if this person feels upset, that you must feel the same way in order to demonstrate your concern and caring for the other individual. If I am in a happy mood, I can feel compassion for you, without having to change my own feeling tone.

In a good relationship each individual will respect the wishes of the other the vast majority of the time, However, there will, in rare instances, be times when one needs to look "behind" the person's words and perhaps act differently than requested. One needs to really know his mate to do this successfully.

What our society stereotypically calls a "strong person" is *actually* a "weak person" emotionally. If an individual can cry, feels frightened at times, insecure, angry, jealous, loving, etc., and simply accepts all of these feelings as being *human*, then he is a "strong person" emotionally, in the sense that he is not afraid to be a *genuine human being*.

We can never directly "see" another person's feelings. We can only *infer* it through the individual's *actions* and *words*. Emotionally mature individuals' actions and words *coincide* so it is easy to infer how they are feeling. However, emotionally immature or disturbed people's actions and words often do *not* coincide, leaving us confused as to their true feelings. For example, if the former says, "I love you," his words will be corroborated by "loving" (considerate) actions. In the case of the latter, the words may be "I love you," but the person's actions may be selfish and even mean. This may well confuse the other person.

Teachers, on *all* grade levels require courses on self-awareness and on developing effective relating skills in and out of the classroom.

Many teachers do not attend to the *most* important aspect of being an effective educator. Initially it is to concentrate on creating a learning atmosphere in which the students are excited, stimulated, and feel cared about by the teacher. Ideally they should view the teacher as their educated "teammate" in the learning process.

In my opinion, *every* teacher, besides knowing his material, *must* have good mental health, and solid relating skills in order to work in his field. It is the *right* of every student, whether he gets an "A" or an "F," to expect his teacher to possess the emotional and social skills to serve as a model in these areas.

There will be times in a relationship when you are very distressed with your partner's behavior. However, sometimes, in these instances, it is obvious that the person fully comprehends what he has done to upset you, and feels very badly about it. In these cases, it is *caring* and *wise* to *not* pursue the matter anymore. Isn't it sad, though, how many of us need to make our mate "suffer" a little more in these instances.

There are really two types of tiredness: emotional and physical. One way of testing out which is the case at any given moment is exercise. If someone is emotionally tired, and he exercises, he will tend to feel rejuvenated, and he will wake up. If, on the other hand, he is physically tired, exercise will just increase his level of tiredness. This differentiation explains the fairly common occurrence where an individual feels "too tired" to have sex with his mate; yet, after a couple of minutes of foreplay is now "wide awake." In this instance, the person was initially emotionally tired. (P.S. — the next time someone asks you to go out, and you want to, but feel too tired, you might test the above out; wake up; and end up having a *great* time.)

Many people complain that their mate does not satisfy them sexually. When the reason or reasons for this are discussed, it is apparent that a "Houdini effect" is at the core of the problem; namely, one or both members expect their partner to "read their minds" in terms of knowing what satisfies them sexually. The remedy for this, of course, is open, frank, and gentle verbal communication with respect to each person's lovemaking needs.

Many people will go to great lengths so as not to experience painful or angry feelings. Alcoholism, other types of drug abuse, sleeping too much, and avoidance of other people are common examples of nonproductive, and in some cases, self-destructive techniques utilized by some individuals who do not want to feel certain emotions.

If an individual makes a statement about another person's personality that the latter knows and accepts as being true, then typically *no* extreme response will ensue. Similarly, if an individual makes a remark that the other person knows is false (e.g. – "You are stupid"), again, typically, no intense response will occur. However, I have witnessed some extremely hostile responses when individual "A" makes a statement about individual "B's" personality that the latter knows "down deep" *is* true, but *cannot* accept.

It is important that parents convey through their words and actions a *realistic* view of life to their children as well as a *realistic* view of how they view their children.

We must never forget, that as parents, we have the responsibility, whenever possible, to expose our children and ourselves to the *beauty* and *magic* of life.

Children learn to relate to others, not only as a function of how their parents treat them, but also as a function of how the parents treat *each other*, as well as other people. For example, the father who is continuously abusing his wife on a physical and/or emotional level, is teaching his children how a man should treat a woman. Similarly, the mother, who is receiving this abuse is also teaching her children how a woman should relate to a man. This educative process within the family will have a tremendous impact on the child's self-image and relating skills.

It is both astonishing and frightening to me that a number of psychiatrists, psychologists, and other types of therapists have such poor mental health, and also exhibit poor relating skills. This has often lead me to believe that the field of psychotherapy, in some instances, attracts the very people who are among the *least* suited emotionally and socially to be effective therapists.

There is a "child" inside of each of us. It consists of the fun loving, spontaneous, wonderous, "bubbly" parts of our personality. Emotionally mature individuals never lose touch with the "child" inside of them. They also know when to express the "child" in them, and when not to. I have noted in my therapy practice that many people with emotional problems (e.g. — depressed and obsessive individuals) have lost contact with this wonderful, vital component of their personality. For the therapy to be successful, they must regain contact with the "child" that resides in all of us throughout our lifetime.

Some people keep "checklists" of what they do for you. They will often throw it up to you if you are angry with their behavior. This is unfair and unloving, as feelings do not work on the basis of "checklists." There is also an element of "emotional blackmail" in this behavior.

Too many people lead a boring, depriving, *defensive* type of life. They are constantly looking out for a "rainy" day. They are preoccupied with the future as much as 20, 30 or even 40 years hence. They hoard their money as the squirrels do their nuts. These people have not been taught that while it is important to live with some foresight and planning, it is *most* important to *enjoy* the present. In many instances, at the core of this problem, are deep feelings of fearfulness and mistrustfulness.

Aerobic exercise (e.g. — running, swimming) is a wonderful remedy for coping with occasional mild anxiety and/or depression. It *certainly* is superior to the unconscionable practice of some psychiatrists and other medical doctors who write prescriptions for anti-anxiety drugs (e.g. — Valium, Librium) which are very addicting, for the same symptoms. It is my firm belief that if a medical doctor prescribes such drugs, then it *must* be accompanied with a recommendation for individual psychotherapy, as the drug will simply eliminate symptoms, not eliminate the *cause* of the symptoms.

It is important to remember that in a relationship each individual can never constitute more than 50% of that relationship. Therefore, I may very much desire a certain type of relationship with another person, but if that person does not want this, then it will not occur as I had desired.

An important saying applicable to relating is that an individual cannot keep kicking you in the rear unless *you keep bending over*, (i.e. — Client: "My boyfriend is so mean to me." Therapist: "How long have you been seeing each other?" Client: "Three years!").

I have felt for a long time that if a man does not have, and he does not ask a woman prior to intercourse if she has proper contraceptives, then the woman should not go to bed with him. Why? If he has so little regard for her becoming pregnant, why should she share something special and pleasurable with him?

If an individual does not experience a loving childhood, he will forever long to attain it. When the same person becomes a parent, he may expect his child to "mother" him, or become a jealous and competitive rival with his child as a result. I have seen many cases of this in and out of therapy, where a parent really does not have the emotional capacity for "parenting" as he did not receive it himself from *his* parents.

When you add a person to your life (e.g. – girlfriend, husband), you are *certainly* adding to the frustrations you will experience. However, you also are providing yourself with the *opportunity* to experience heightened emotional pleasures and satisfactions, in essence, the opportunity for an *enriched* life.

I have witnessed a number of cases, in and out of therapy, where a child has become the victim, or designated "sick one" of the family. In reality, the problem stems from the parents harboring considerable animosity *toward one another*, and are venting their wrath onto the child. I have found many times, that the "sick child" is actually the *healthiest* member of the family!

Many people do not understand that you can love someone very much, be attracted to that person, and yet experience sexual feelings toward other people. These feelings do not make the individual any less faithful or loving toward his mate, and do not indicate that there is a problem in the relationship. Rather, these feelings simply reflect the biologically based sexual drive that we all possess. Emotionally mature individuals simply enjoy these sexual feelings whenever they arise, accepting them like any other feelings, and not acting on them.

When you are feeling depressed, a good question to ask yourself is: "Am I angry at somebody or some event, and am I turning this anger on myself?"

Emotionally healthy individuals are quite accurate in sizing up their environment, and thinking logically. However, less healthy individuals tend to misperceive situations, and to think illogically. They may tend, for example, to provoke the wrath of others through their words and actions, yet only bemoan how they are being mistreated, totally unaware of their hostile or selfish provocations. Often times, this individual has "modeled" himself after one or both of his parents. I have observed this behavior in *many* individuals.

Individuals who have emotional and thinking problems often tend to see another person's behavior or an environmental event as being due to the latter's reaction to the disturbed individual. In essence, if I do not immediately smile when I see this person, I *must* be angry with him. If the train is an hour late, this was done deliberately to punish the individual. This tendency to *personalize* other people's behavior and environmental events tends to cause *all* kinds of relating problems for the individual, and those he comes in contact with. It also is typically exhibited by at least one other family member, particularly a parent.

It is a sign of emotional maturity to be able to enjoy another person's accomplishments and/or good fortune.

Some psychologists, psychiatrists and other therapists are so into looking at the deficiencies and "defects" of their clients, that they forget to look at their strengths. This does nothing to enhance the self-image of the client, and needlessly prolongs the therapy.

The famous psychiatrist, Dr. Sigmund Freud, the founder of psychoanalysis, believed that sex was the major psychological and biological drive in human beings. Over the years, as a close observer of all kinds of relationships, I have *not* found this to be the case. Rather, the primary motivating drive in people is the need to be *loved*.

If an individual cares about you, or even loves you, and you do not feel the same way, then you have an *obligation* and a *duty* to be gentle with the person. (This does *not* mean that you have to force yourself—even if you could—to feel the same way.) I have seen too many cases where the less involved individual callously dismisses, or even is cruel to the more involved person. Remember, this person is potentially a friend or lover for *someone else* who *will* feel as intensely as they do, and you do not want to damage the person for future loving relationships.

People who are experiencing sexual functioning difficulties are not often aware that, in many (but not all) cases, the specific sexual dysfunction does not reflect an underlying biological problem, but rather is due to the person's great fear of getting *physically and emotionally close to another person*.

I respect people who state that they do not want to get married or are married and choose not to have children, because they believe that they are too selfish or too self-centered. These people are aware of their limitations and accept them. As a result, they will not emotionally abuse a child by periodically stating how good life would have been if the child had never been born.

The most basic right that every child is entitled to is that his parents provide the child with an environment where the child feels *protected, safe,* and *secure*.

It would be very beneficial if all couples who planned to get married were required to go for a few counseling sessions in order to help determine whether each is emotionally mature enough for matrimony, including understanding the responsibilities and stresses as well as the joys and pleasures found in marriages. This procedure would help prevent a lot of grief and pain from occurring.

Many people are so frightened of life and of living that they spend their entire life trying to control everyone and everything around them. This often reflects a lack of trust in themselves and in the world, and stems from a neglectful and/or abusive early parenting experience or experiences as a child. These same people present themselves to others as being "strongwilled and competent." In reality, it is a mirage: these people actually feel *extremely insecure* and *dependent* underneath.

If an individual is having difficulty relating to a family member or friend, the disagreement should *remain* between these two people. I have seen all too many times where one or more individuals in this situation have callously and selfishly "bad mouthed" the other person in an attempt to turn family and/or friends against the latter.

If an individual begins to tell you negative things about someone you know, this person is exhibiting a lack of respect and caring for the person being criticized as well as for *you*. There is also an element of cowardice being demonstrated by this type of behavior, as well as manipulativeness.

There is a definite relationship between how an individual feels about himself and how tolerant this person is of, and how he treats, other people. Therefore, if someone is being cold or criticizing you for no apparent reason, ask the individual how he is feeling about himself.

It is very common in our society for an individual who is in "a bad mood" to feel free to throw all social amenities "out the window." If you ask such a person why he is acting this way, he will typically state that he is in this bad mood. It is *imperative* in order to maintain one's self-respect and out of self-caring to not allow such a person to continue to act in this callous, uncaring manner to you.

When I am going to refer an individual to another therapist for psychotherapy, I will always pick the therapist who demonstrates the *best relating skills and emotional health* in relating to *me*.

If you want an individual to "tune you out" (not listen to you), then talk in terms of absolutes such as "always" or "never." Very few occurrences in life warrant using either of these terms. If you want a person to listen to you, be *precise* in your statements (i.e. — "you sometimes. . . . . .," "you occasionally. . . . . .," "you often. . . . .," as opposed to "you always. . . . . .," or "you never. . . . . .").

In a relationship, when an individual expresses anger over the behavior of the other, the latter should not "retaliate" by bringing up a past grievance or grievances. The ensuing conversation needs to focus on the *present* problem.

One way of looking at psychotherapy is that it is a process by which the client becomes emotionally independent of the therapist. Another way to look at it, is that therapy is successfully completed when the therapist has become *irrelevant* in the client's life. Why is this? It is because the client is now able to "let go" of the therapist, and can now find his own satisfactions.

It is my opinion that being an effective therapist is roughly one third due to the therapist's training and credentials (i.e. – clinical psychologist, psychiatrist), and approximately two thirds due to the therapist's emotional health, sensitivity, perceptiveness, and level of relating skills. A therapist requires *both* components in order to be effective.

In general, there is little relationship between the fee a therapist charges and the quality and effectiveness of the therapy.

Beware of therapists who try to *undermine* your attempts at eventually becoming emotionally independent of them. These therapists certainly believe in "long term therapy." These individuals will tend to encourage their clients to check with them before making all decisions: they keep pointing out how much you need the therapy, and they are quick to point out "the dangers" of leaving the therapy prematurely. Of course, I am not talking about the minority of cases where the client is seriously or severely emotionally disturbed. To me, these "therapists" (and there are far too many of them) are simply unscrupulous and badly require therapy for themselves.

I believe that psychotherapy can only progress to the degree of emotional health and to the level of relating skills of the *therapist*. Since psychotherapy basically involves the emotional and social *re-education* of the client, the "teacher" can only re-educate the "student" (client) up to the teacher's development in both of these areas.

Many parents do not understand what their relationship should be with respect to their children. In essence, parents are the emotional and social educators of their children.

Parents who can laugh at themselves and, in general, do not take themselves too seriously, will tend to have children who feel relatively comfortable in relating to these parents. In contrast, I have seen all too many parents who are so into their children "respecting" them that this overrides all other aspects of the parent-child relationship. In general, I have found such parents to be pompous, unloving, and selfish. They obviously had never been taught that love and respect have to be *earned* through loving and respectful *actions*, rather than because someone is given the title "mother" or "father."

Without a doubt, the field of psychotherapy is *both* an *art* as well as a *science*.

It is *very* good for a relationship to do what I like to call "keeping in touch." This means that one or the other member of the couple will periodically sit his mate down, and inquire: "How is life for you?"; "Are you happy?"; "How have you been feeling toward me?"; and "How are you feeling toward our relationship?" The motivation here does *not* stem from insecurity. Rather, it stems from *caring* about oneself, one's partner, and the relationship.

It is a sad commentary on our society how unaffectionate we tend to be toward one another. This partly stems from observing how affectionate or unaffectionate our parents were toward us, each other, and other people. It is apparently also due to the fact that many people cannot discriminate between being affectionate, and being sexual. Emotionally mature individuals can generally differentiate when they are behaving affectionately (i.e. − a kiss on the cheek), and when they are behaving sexually (i.e. − a kiss flush on the mouth). They know what their *motivation* is when they seek physical contact with another human being. On the other hand, emotionally immature individuals tend to either shun all physical contact, or almost always are seductive when they relate physically to another person.

In a significant number of marriages, one or both members have "mistresses," but these "mistresses" are *not* necessarily other people. Rather, they consist of any activity or activities which one of the partners places in importance *above* the relationship. A good example of this is *work*. There are a significant number of husbands who are rarely home because they are working (I am not talking about the cases where there is a *genuine* economic necessity for this behavior). These "workaholics," while quite acceptable in our society, in actuality, have their priorities reversed. This state of "affairs" (unbeknownst to most people) suggests marked problems in the relationship, and suggests a greater tendency for a *human* mistress or mistresses to eventually occur.

The more emotionally healthy an individual is, the better this person is at getting his needs met in a socially acceptable way.

Many individuals appear to have a great deal of difficulty in paying another human being a *genuine* compliment. Many of these same people have received few sincere compliments from the key people in their lives. In some cases, they may also feel that by paying another individual a genuine compliment that they are taking something away from, or in some cases, are "lowering" themselves. In fact, it is a *wonderful* thing to be able to pay another human being a sincere compliment. The "senders" (if emotionally healthy) will most likely experience a feeling of emotional freedom and openness, and the "receiver" (if emotionally healthy) will tend to feel cared about and respected. In essence, each individual as well as the relationship will benefit from genuine compliments.

Many psychologists and philosophers have invested considerable energy in trying to determine whether people are born inherently "good" or "bad." In my opinion, they are born *neither*. Human beings are born with *needs*. It is of paramount importance that society, including parents, teach children how to meet these needs as best as possible in a socially acceptable manner. If society fulfills its responsibility, it will create "good human beings."

If you want a quick way to determine how an individual's self-image is (the way one feels about oneself), pay the person a sincere compliment. I have seen many individuals who are treated this way either respond by acting as if the sender had never said it at all (the proverbial "in one ear and out the other"), had embarrassed the individual, or even insulted the individual. On the other hand, mildly criticize the same individual, and the person seems to take this comment to heart. In essence, the person with the poor self-image cannot accept genuine compliments because of the incongruency between his self-image and the statement. On the other hand, a critical statement can be accepted and assimilated because it goes along with the person's self-image. People with a good or positive self-image can readily accept, and are obviously pleased when receiving a genuine compliment.

Emotionally mature individuals are not preoccupied with "achievement" in bed. While it surely is a loving thing to experience an orgasm or orgasms, to make the latter the "goal" of lovemaking, is to take away the fun and spontaneity of the experience. In essence, emotionally mature individuals are into the quality of their own and their partner's *feelings*.

I have noted over the years that when a member of a family comes for individual psychotherapy, then the *entire* family will be affected by this learning experience. This is because each family appears to have a set of "implicit" as well as "explicit" rules for each family member to follow. The result of this is a balance being established for each family constellation. When an individual begins to make progress in the therapy, he will begin to relate differently to family members, and the existing balance will be threatened. Initially, the other family members will tend to "fight" to maintain the present situation. However, if the individual therapy is effective, there will be a new equilibrium established which will have beneficial effects for some or all of the other family members, as well as for the client being treated.

I have felt for a long time that a therapist will tend to be more effective, other things being equal, if he has a part-time rather than a full-time practice. If one simply has a full-time psychotherapy job, there is a *much greater* possibility of emotional "burn-out," and there is a greater financial influence on the therapist if a client wants to leave (of course, I am aware that some therapists have very large practices where the latter is not a problem , but the "burn-out" issue is very much the case).

If an individual keeps accusing you of being unfaithful without any justification, then it may well be that this person is actually putting his *own* sexual feelings, fantasies, and even behavior onto you.

48

Just because an individual is a "great friend," it does *not* necessarily follow that he is a comparable father, daughter, brother, etc. In fact, I have treated a number of individuals who had a relative who was actually cruel to his family, yet was a well-liked friend. In essence, if I have a given view of a person based on my experience with him, I must respect that someone else may have a completely different view of this same individual due to entirely different experiences with him. I have witnessed some damaging arguments between a husband and wife, because one party kept insisting how "wonderful" a given person is, thus negating the other individual's perceptions, and feelings, evoking hurtful and resentful feelings as a consequence.

Some people are so dependent on their partner that they are willing to put up with almost any indignity at the hands of the latter. These same individuals actually believe that by "turning the other cheek" they are preserving the integrity of their relationship. In actuality, they are doing just the *opposite*. They are actually encouraging their mate to go to greater lengths in neglecting and/or abusing them, and in doing so, ever *increasing* the probability that the abusive individual will eventually leave them.

It certainly is a wonderful gift that children have such a capacity for *enjoying* themselves. It is one of the *great* tasks for parents, in particular, and for society, in general, to preserve this capacity, in the process of molding a "socially acceptable" human being. It is such a sad commentary that so many individuals are beset with worries and fears, that they can never or almost never fully enjoy a special moment or moments.

There are families where one parent consistently "bad mouths" the other parent to the children, filling their heads with distortions and even downright lies. This parent sets himself up as the family "information center" (and is allowed to do so), telling each family member how insensitive and hostile each person in the family is. At the same time, this parent communicates the message that he is the only family member who "really" cares about each person within the family. This type of cruel and manipulative behavior has done great damage to many families, and resulted in the separation and hatred between family members. I have experienced great pleasure and satisfaction in helping a client to clearly see this type of disturbed behavior and to help correct it.

Many of us harbor the false assumption that if an individual is upset or angry about something that the only way to relieve these tensions is to start screaming. In actuality, these tensions can normally be alleviated if the same individual shares his thoughts and feelings in an honest and frank manner. I have seen a number of "yellers" in therapy, who were absolutely amazed in discovering the truth of this statement.

I strongly believe that every individual would greatly benefit from living in his own apartment for one or two years. This would force the individual to become self-sufficient and increase his self-confidence. If this person subsequently chooses to live with another person, he knows this is based on *caring* rather than on *dependency*. Also, this individual is aware that if the relationship does not work, he can definitely cope. Finally, if you have, over a period of time, done all the chores required of an adult, you will much more likely *appreciate* the other person's contributions to the relationship (i.e. – cooking, paying bills, earning a living, etc.).

Many people do not understand the difference between being *assertive*, and being *hostilely aggressive*. An individual who is being assertive is simply standing up for his rights. If you are waiting on line in a bakery, and it is your turn, and someone speaks up, then stating firmly that it is your turn, is both appropriate and self-respectful, in essence, being assertive. On the other hand, if I am waiting for someone to pull out of a parking lot spot, and another individual suddenly zooms right into it, this is being hostilely aggressive, which is entirely inappropriate as well as antisocial. It is very important that parents teach their children this distinction early in life because it will help them throughout their lifetimes.

It is very important to allow your children to make *mistakes*: the child who almost never makes a mistake is not experimenting and experiencing life fully enough. They have been taught to take a very cautious, safe "small slice of life." If a child periodically makes a reasonable mistake, his parents should not "make a big deal" out of this. Instead, they should state that mistakes are part of life, and they are part of the learning process and, therefore, a valuable part of the child's development. In general, I have found that parents who "went crazy" whenever their children made a mistake, could not admit when they *themselves* ever made an error. This is a sorry state of affairs because when we make a mistake, we are simply being human.

It is a wonderful thing to share *relevant, age-appropriate* experiences with your child. If the child is having difficulty with a teacher, and the parent determines that it is the teacher, and not the child that is at fault, then it may well help the child by telling him about a similar experience that might have happened to you, the parent. This will tend to help your child feel closer to you: feel more accepted and normal, and encourage the child to be more "open" in talking to the parent.

It is often asked, "How can I get to know how someone really is, who I have just started to date?" In essence, an individual can probably learn more about another person's personality by focusing on how this individual treats *others* on the date, more so than how he treats you. For example, the person in question may be quite gracious and thoughtful in his relating to you, but will be ill-mannered to a waiter, or drive in a selfish, callous manner on the highway. These latter behaviors must not be ignored and should serve as a "warning" of how this individual can potentially treat *you.*

Many parents make the mistake of doing too much for their children. They will literally "rush" to their child's aid, if the child shows the slightest inability to complete a task (i.e. — button a shirt, cook a meal) in the name of being a helpful "good" parent. In reality, what this behavior pattern does is *undermine* the child's feelings of competency, self-confidence, and self-liking. The child is getting the "message" from his parents that "you need me to do things for you, because you are unable to cope adequately." In essence, parents need to let their children do as much for themselves as is reasonable for the child's age, and if the child cannot do it, then the parent should try to help the child so the child *can* do it for himself.

It is very common to hear an individual say, 'You made me feel. . . . .'' This assumes that another person is *responsible* for how we are feeling. This is an untrue statement. Individual "A" may say or do something in individual "B's" presence, and the latter will feel *whatever* he will feel. If one individual's behavior really did cause feelings to occur in another person, then it would follow that if I tell you that you are looking very well, then you should *always* feel the *same* feeling whenever I say this to you. In reality if I tell you that you are looking well, depending upon many independent factors occurring internally, and externally, in your private life, you may on one occasion smile and say "Thank you;" and on another, exhibit no overt reaction; and on a third occasion, actually scream that you do not, and tell me off. In general, people who tend to speak in terms of "you made me feel" statements, also tend to provoke guilt in others with these and similar statements and actions. They may also tend to be overly dependent, and even parasitic in their relationships.

It is an expecially pleasurable thing to watch someone who *really enjoys* what he does for a living. When this is the case, the job usually allows the person considerable *self-expression*.

It would enhance parent-child relating, if parents did not tell their children that they were "good boys," "good girls," "bad boys," or "bad girls." Why is this? This is because children tend to translate a parent saying, "Drew, you are a good boy" into "Drew, I love you;" while "Drew, you are a bad boy," is interpreted to mean, "Drew, I do not love you." Such statements can have adverse effects on the development of the child's self-image and feelings of loveableness or unloveableness.

It is of primary importance that parents teach their children that *parents,* just like their children, are *human beings,* with rights, feelings, and needs. Some children are never taught this by their parents, and as a result view their mother and father as "Santa Claus." This development will have serious implications for both the child and his parents as the child will tend to become self-centered, selfish, callous, infantile, dependent, omnipotent, and overly demanding. As for the parents, they will never complete their raising of this child; he will remain dependent and even parasitic on them for the remainder of their days; a sad state of affairs for the child and his parents.

I have found that most effective therapists share the following personality traits: *warmth* and *humility.*

If an individual has experienced neglect and/or abuse at the hands of a family member early in life, then this person will walk around with "emotional wounds" which will make this individual sensitized to certain individuals and certain situations. If you are in a situation where you believe that your feelings are too intense for what is happening at the moment, or you do not understand why you are feeling the way you do, then it is a wise thing to consider that perhaps the present situation is a catalyst for releasing pent-up feelings that have festered for years in these "emotional wounds." It is a wonderful thing to be able to discriminate when your feelings are simply related to what is happening at the moment, versus feelings that are largely coming from past experiences. An individual who *is* aware that the latter is occurring should simply keep these feelings to himself, and in this manner not "take out" on an innocent person, feelings which have little or nothing to do with this individual. This will help keep your relationship alive and well. For example, if my wife asks if I would mind if she buys a half dozen roses, and I suddenly find myself unaccountably feeling very angry over this innocent request, knowing that these feelings are probably related to a past family member, I would keep these feelings to myself: accept them, and simply say "Fine."

It is a worthwhile venture to periodically *"take stock"* of one's life. Are we happy with our life; what can be done to enhance it, etc. So many of us are so into "perpetual motion" that we never stop and take a real look at the *quality* of our existence.

There are many people who are rushing to get that degree; to buy that house; to earn that promotion, in order to finally feel happy. However, all too often once they attain this goal, they are dismayed to note that they still feel the same or even worse! In essence, these individuals, while professing to running *toward* what will make them happy, are actually running *away* from their feelings and *from themselves*. Only by taking a look at "their inner world" through therapy, for example, can a significant emotional change occur.

If parents want to determine how good their adolescent child's self-image is, they can simply observe whom he chooses for friends, and especially whom he "falls in love" with.

It is becoming more and more apparent that it is crucial that parents establish clear, concrete *"Rules of the House"* as well as clearly state for their child what the *consequences* will be for different types of behavior. I have seen a number of children in therapy whose parents, while being very sensitive to their feelings, and opinions, have *not* provided a consistent pattern of disciplining, along with a workable set of "Rules" that they expect their child to follow. As a result, these children are tending to misbehave in school, at home, and in other social situations.

With more and more theories appearing, dealing with how to raise emotionally healthy children, the most important aspect involves *quality time*. Every child needs a certain amount of time spent with each parent where the parents actively relate to, invest effort in, and emotionally as well as socially educate the child. So many people are so into their own careers and themselves, that they do not provide the child either with the *quality of care* or the *time* required for good child rearing (P.S. — this may go against the genre of the times, but if people do not want to put the time into raising their children, and both individuals want to pursue careers, then fine; *don't* have children).

If a child has experienced neglect and/or abuse at the hands of one or both parents, then he will have a tendency, emotionally, to treat his children in a neglectful and/or abusive manner. In some instances, this pattern of behavior may *not* manifest itself until the child is older, an adolescent, or even an adult.

I have witnessed some individuals in and out of therapy do some of the most rejecting, hostile things in the name of *pride* and *principle*.

58

A significant number of people in our society suffer from what I like to call, "money sickness." These individuals appear to be primarily motivated by accruing as much money as fast as possible, and they are all consumed when it comes to this matter. Many of these people are very insecure: lack faith in the future, and suffer from deep feelings of "emotional emptiness." It is sad that they will never accrue enough money to fill up this emotional void, as we can never fill the latter by accumulating money. What these people *really* need is a good therapy experience.

It is quite common in our society to hear people talk about how they are going to *change their partner* in a relationship. On one level, this is an *arrogant* position, as the person is implying that he *knows* what is "best" for the other individual. Also, the person is not considering the "rights" and "feelings" of the other individual as she or he may *not* want to change (which is *any* person's right). In essence, if there are minor differences between two people who are relating, and the two are *willing* and *able* to change, then the relationship should prosper. On the other hand, if there are *major* differences between the two people (i.e. — one member believes in an "open" marriage, the other does not), then the most reasonable solution would be to end the relationship.

There are times in a relationship, where both people feel "emotionally drained." They have little or no emotional resources available to nurture themselves let alone their mate. In these instances, it is important that each member of the relationship be "in touch" with this fact, and openly discuss it with one another. In such cases, it is very beneficial if the couple engage in activities where a *third* party nurtures both of *them*, such as eating dinner out; going to an entertaining movie or play, or any other emotionally *replenishing* activity.

The best therapists do *not* "hide" behind a therapy approach, rigidly adhering to the principles of Freud, or Rogers, or Ellis, and the like. These therapists study the various therapeutic perspectives, and take what seems most beneficial and effective in helping their clients to grow. *These* excellent therapists are well aware that much more than any theoretical or therapeutic perspective, that the major asset that they present in the therapy situation is *themselves*. One of the attractive traits of these therapists is that they take *responsibility* for what they do in the therapy, rather than putting the "onus" on the approach they follow, or its inventor.

Sexual relating is a wonderful avenue for expressing one's creativity, spontaneity, and for having a lot of fun.

There are many people in our society who seem to "love" to *judge* other individual's behavior. They are constantly saying such things as, "I never would have done it that way."; or "I could never say such a thing."; or "How could he have done such a thing?" This type of behavior will tend to effectively distance, and "turn off" others to this arrogant, critical individual. It is also interesting that many of the behaviors that this person criticizes, he actually exhibits *himself*.

People sometimes ask, "What is the best way for me to conduct myself sexually?" In actuality, there are *many* sexual lifestyles which are perfectly acceptable. Within this diversity, the one that is for you, is the one where you will feel *best* about *yourself* as a *self-respecting human being*.

Many people are involved with what is the "right" frequency of sex for a couple. Contrary to many popular publications, the "right" frequency of sex is what best meets the *needs* of the two people involved. Using this rationale, a couple engaging in sexual behavior once every ten days could be having as good a sex life *for them*, as for a couple having sexual relations four or five times a week. It's all a matter of needs being met in a compatible manner.

A common complaint of couples is that they are *bored*. In some cases, this does *not* reflect any real problem with the relationship. Rather, each individual is basically bored with *himself*. If I am bored with myself, and my personal life, it is going to be *very* difficult for me not to be bored with everyone else, including my mate, as well as with my relationship.

Sometimes when couples complain that they are *bored,* this *does* indeed reflect serious problems in the relationship. Here, the individuals have tended to try to ignore "or push out of their minds" hurts and animosities that have accumulated over the weeks, months, or even years at the hands of their partner. This follows the adage, that the opposite of love is not hate; it is *apathy*. These couples require intensive marriage counseling or therapy, if they are to have a chance to rekindle the caring feelings which formerly existed.

It is of primary importance in a relationship for both parties to be able to put themselves in their mate's place; to feel what the latter is feeling, and to be able to empathize with the person's perceptions, as well as to be able to comprehend how life is for our mate in his daily living. If both people can do this, this will definitely enhance the *quality* and *caring* of the relationship.

When two individuals have invested a lot of time, energy, and caring in a relationship, it is only decent, that if one member feels very dissatisfied with it; or actually wants to *end* the relationship, then he should talk to his mate about seeking counseling or therapy. I have seen too many cases where one individual leaves the other without making any real effort in correcting the problems that exist. In these instances, I have heard their mate painfully and bitterly bemoan that, "I feel as if I was flushed down the toilet." In essence, out of respect for your mate, the relationship, and yourself, professional counseling or psychotherapy should be tried. If this fails, that is all any couple can do.

Too many individuals in our society are too quick to stereotype people, and even stigmatize them because of advancing age. In reality, age has little to do with one's capacity to experience and enjoy life, and to function as a productive human being. As we grow older, however, society often sets up obstacles to hinder our development as complete human beings (i.e. — mandatory retirement; a professional ballplayer is "over the hill" as he approaches the age of *40, regardless* of his present level of performance, etc.). In reality, it is the "slice of life" we take each year which *really* determines whether we are "young" or "old." Using this criterion, there are many "youthful" *80* year olds and many "old" *20* year olds.

It is common conception that divorce in our society is synonymous with "failure." This is not always the case. Sometimes, over the years people change in different ways; that is, the two individuals grow in disparate directions. What was satisfactory in a relationship 10, 20, 30 or even more years ago, is no longer adequate for one or both members of the relationship. In these cases, a resulting divorce does *not* indicate a "failure," but rather that both people no longer adequately are getting their needs met now, as compared to the past.

In the majority of cases, a divorce signifies that one or both members of the relationship did and do not possess the *degree of emotional health*, as well as the *level of relating skills* necessary to make the relationship a mutually satisfying and enjoyable one. If either or both parties is to subsequently have a better relationship, then it is imperative that they either go for counseling or psychotherapy to understand their deficits in these areas and correct them if they are ever going to have a mature, emotionally satisfying relationship with someone else.

With all the courses offered an individual throughout his academic career, it amazes me that there is not a course on self-understanding, and developing solid relating skills at every level of schooling, starting at the elementary school level, and progressing yearly through the junior high, and high school years. This "education" may prove to be the most important as the individual will utilize it throughout his entire life.

It is becoming more and more apparent, that there is a great need to educate people on what it means to be someone's mother versus their wife, and father versus their husband. Many of us do not understand that our wife is *not* our mother, and that our husband is *not* our father. I have seen case after case of troubled relationships, where a major problem existed because either or both parties did not emotionally and/or intellectually understand these differentiations and, as a result, each person harbored unrealistic expectations of the other. In fact, I have heard on a number of occasions a husband attempting to belittle his wife by saying, "You won't do this for me? My mother would have.", or a wife stating, "You know, you are not like my father" (in a critical tone).

Many of us do not understand the difference between feeling "jealous," and feeling "envious." For example, if you win a trip to Paris, and I resent that you won it, when I feel that I should have won this trip, then my underlying feeling is one of jealousy. On the other hand, if you win a trip to Paris, and I genuinely am happy for you, but I *also* would like to win the same trip, then my underlying feeling is one of envy.

It takes much less energy to try to get along with people, generally, than it does to be at odds with them.

Especially in this society, it is crucial that our child develop good, solid inner *values*. As parents, our words in this area will have some impact on our children. However, the way we conduct ourselves, and live our lives will be of far more import, in terms of how our children behave, and in terms of the values they develop within.

It is not uncommon to hear parents tell their children that they expect them to get "A's" or "90's" on their report cards, and if the children do not attain these types of grades, they may well be criticized. This practice is unloving as well as unfair. The *only* thing that a parent can justifiably expect from his child academically is that he *try hard*. Given all the variables that go into getting a particular grade, and the fact that very few children, and/or adolescents are equally adept in all subjects, it is unrealistic to expect a given level of academic achievement in all areas. The only thing a child or adolescent can do is make a good effort, and it is this effort or lack of effort, that parents need to reward or discipline. In essence, whether my child attains "A's" or "D's," if he has made a good effort, that is all I can ask.

When a parent announces that his young child is definitely going to be a professional, such as a lawyer, I immediately ask that parent when *he* is going to begin law school. Children are in this world to be raised, educated, and loved. They are *not* in this world to make up for the parents' own frustrations. In essence, children are not to be *exploited* by their parents' own selfish desires.

There are situations where two or more individuals that you care about, or even love, are at odds. In these situations,the loving posture is to *stay out* of the turmoil, allowing the involved parties to work it out themselves, or for them to go for professional counseling or therapy if this is not feasible. I have witnessed too many instances, where the individual will take sides, totally rejecting one person, and aligning oneself with the other. This type of behavior is usually *not* based on any fair or rational basis. Rather, this individual will tend to side with the person *he is more dependent upon*, whether or not this person is obviously being unfair or even abusive. For example, a son will tend to blindly side with his mother against his sister, even if it is obvious that the mother is being insensitive to the point of cruelty to the sister. Emotionally mature individuals will continue to be loving to *both* sides, not allowing either to pressure him to pick one person or the other, and refusing to listen to any "badmouthing" of any of the people involved.

It is important to realize that there are some very disturbed people in our society who cannot be reasoned with. It is wise to keep this in mind when someone is disrespectful of your rights. If you are dealing with someone who is severely mentally ill (i.e. — psychotic), your first priority should be not to have a confrontation with such an individual, but to handle the situation without evoking an unpredictable, violent or bizarre reaction. In essence, these people need to be handled with all due tact.

Many people assume that if an individual is not behaving appropriately, then there *must* be some *aberration* or *defect* at the core of this behavior. While this *is* sometimes the case, there are many instances where the person's inappropriate behavior is *not* due to any innate defect but rather reflects an *immaturity* in the person's emotional and social development. As such, the individual is behaving this way because he has not progressed in these realms beyond a level of emotional and social development appropriate for an infant or young child. For example, if an individual's father throws a violent temper tantrum when mildly frustrated, this behavior may well reflect an *immaturity* factor (namely, functioning emotionally and socially like a two or three year old) rather than being due to any defect or aberration (although in some cases it might). When this is indeed the case, and the individual correctly views his father's behavior as being like a little child, it becomes not only understandable, but much less intimidating and frightening, and there is now hope of the person being able to cope with such immature behavior.

There are a goodly number of people in our society who are extremely selfish. These narcissistic individuals tend to find it very difficult to understand *another* person's situation, including their thoughts and feelings. The best way of reaching such an individual is to relate your experience by using a past or present experience, in the narcissist's life. I have seen a number of these people progress from initially not seeming to comprehend at all what is being told to them, to a real emotional awareness, when an example relevant to their *own* life is presented.

If therapy is successful, then *both* the therapist and the client will be *enriched* by the experience.

There are many individuals in our society who suffer from various levels of depression. A number of them have gone for individual counseling or psychotherapy, once, twice or even three times a week in order to cure this problem. It is my opinion that since depression can be caused by biochemical factors as well as environmental events, that before any counseling or therapy is instituted, that the person go for a complete *physical examination*, in order to rule out any biological basis for his depression. For marked depressions there are a number of anti-depressant drugs which can be a valuable adjunct to the therapy, and can alleviate a lot of unnecessary pain and discomfort.

The *quality* and *frequency* of sex in a relationship is a sensitive indicator of what is happening within and what is happening in an individual's life *outside* of the relationship.

In some instances, a relationship between two people can be as strong as ever, even though the quality and/or frequency of the sex has decreased recently. For example, one or both individuals can be under a lot of pressure at the job; may be studying for final exams, or is very worried about an ill parent. As a result, the person's sex drive is low because of any of these types of stresses, yet, the person may love his mate as much as ever. If this is the case, when the stress or stresses are eliminated, the person or person's sex drive should return, and with it the quality and preferred frequency of sexual behavior.

In some cases, a decrease in the quality and/or frequency of sex, can indeed, indicate that there are problems, and perhaps, even serious problems existing between the two people. When this is the case, usually the individual or individual's sex drive is weakened, as the person tries to cope with underlying feelings (i.e. — hostility, hurt, and/or rejection). The individual harbors these toward his mate. Here, there is a *relationship* problem, *not* merely a sexual difficulty. Some professional counseling or psychotherapy would seem to be indicated here if this situation is to be corrected.

If a couple's sex life is not what it formerly had been, the first step is for the two people to try and sit down to see if they can determine whether there is a problem between the two of them; whether one or both parties is under a lot of stress at the present time, or whether a combination of the two factors exist.

In our society, individuals tend to want to put "blame" on another person, in order to explain why a given mishap has occurred. "Whose fault is it?" often seems to be upper in one or both parties' mind, rather than trying to correct the problem. Emotionally mature individuals are aware that things can happen in life where *no one* is at fault; rather, some mishap occurred, where neither party had any say or control over it happening, or not happening. In essence, finding "fault" or trying to "blame" someone is neither productive nor caring; *correcting the problem* should be the *focus*.

Many people seem preoccupied with what is the "right way" to do something. In a number of instances, there is no "right" or "wrong way." There are simply *different* ways, equally good, at handling the situation.

It is an interesting fact that some therapists refer to the people they see as "patients" while others refer to them as "clients." In my opinion, only a small fraction of the individuals seen for psychotherapy warrant the label "patient." These are the individuals who are suffering from a proven biological disorder which is causing psychological problems as well, and also the relatively small percentage of people who require medication for their psychological disorders. The remaining people who attend psychotherapy, who constitute by far the majority of individuals seen, are essentially *normal* individuals who have some emotional and social difficulties. In essence, these people, if they had been properly educated, would never have required therapy. As such, psychotherapy for them is simply emotional and social re-education. They, therefore, should be referred to as "clients."

Some individuals tend to "hide" behind their professional facade (i.e. − always being "the doctor,"or "the professor"). It is almost as if these people have "no identity" outside of their professional role. This type of behavior generally reflects a "one-sided" development and/or insecurity, as well as a deficiency in the growth of appropriate relating skills.

When a client is about ready to stop coming to therapy, it seems more beneficial for the therapist to tell the client to take a "leave of absence" as opposed to "terminating therapy." This is because many clients, if they want to or have to come back for further therapy, often feel that this means that the original therapy was a "failure" since they have already "terminated" it. On the other hand, "a leave of absence" can simply be viewed as an "infinite" one. I have found this latter approach to be a significantly more fruitful one.

Many therapists do not seem to understand that *nontherapy* issues may be more crucial to the client making significant progress in the experience than what actually transpires within the session. If the client goes into the hospital, and the therapist does not at least call; if the client calls the therapist at home, and is told "tell me at the next session;" or if the therapist refuses to give the client an extra couple of minutes at a particularly important moment (in the client's eyes), then the resulting *damage* to the relationship will more than negate any "brilliant interpretation" or the like made by the therapist. This is because the quality of the therapy *relationship* is the major factor in the success or failure of the therapy.

Emotionally mature individuals can ask another person for help without feeling that such a request "lessens" the worth of the individual. This is because emotionally mature people are aware, and accept, that every person has his assets and his liabilities. Emotionally immature people do one or two things; they either never ask for help or they do the opposite by constantly asking for help.

Many people act as if winning a sporting event, or getting an "A" grade is a life-or-death matter. Other people, while also trying very hard to play well, or get that "A" grade, do *not* make it a "life-or-death" venture. Why is there such a difference? The first type of individual has apparently learned to equate how he performs with how loveable he is as a person, or another way to put it, how worthwhile he is. In essence, this person has a poor self-image, constantly looking for "challenges" to *temporarily* feel good about himself. The second type of individual has a good self-image, therefore, feeling loveable and worthwhile. While he would certainly like to win the sporting event, or get that "A," whether he does or not, will *not* change this person's feelings about himself. This is a major trait of being emotionally mature.

When two individuals plan to get married, it is very beneficial if each party feels what I like to call "*emotionally received*" by their mate's family. This will occur, if each member of the other person's family, through his words and actions conveys the message that "I am glad that you are going to be a member of my family." If this is successfully accomplished, then this will significantly reduce the external stresses placed on the marriage. Unfortunately, I have witnessed many situations where one or both parties to be married felt rejected by the entire family. If you feel this way, then it is imperative that you communicate this to your mate, and the latter needs to try to correct this problem by speaking to his family. If this is accomplished, it will make it much easier for the relationship to proceed smoothly.

One good way of helping an individual feel "emotionally accepted" into your family, is to invite the person to spend time individually with you. Going out for lunch; going shopping together, and the like can be helpful in achieving this goal. If each family member would provide this individual with this type of fruitful time, then there is an excellent chance that the new family member will indeed feel "emotionally accepted" by his mate's family.

If an individual consistently does not want to participate in an activity such as going out socially with friends, or going to Europe on a vacation, it may be that this person is not merely trying to spoil your fun. In many instances, the person may have a *fear* of being with a group of people, or may be frightened about going thousands of miles from home where people may speak another language. It is important, in such cases, that the two people involved have an open, honest talk where the latter can express his fears in a sympathetic environment. Ways of coping with these fears can be sensitively discussed by both parties. I have seen some very bitter arguments occur, when the frightened person did not feel "safe" enough to voice his fears, and the other person simply felt his mate was being selfish and mean for not wanting to participate in the activity being discussed.

Many of us give gifts with "strings" attached. For example, a person gives you a present and then tells you how you *must* use it. Sometimes an individual will give you a present; tell you how much he spent, and mention that "my birthday is coming soon." In essence, when you give someone a gift, it *is* exactly that, something given to another without conditions, including no asking for paybacks or controlling how the gift is to be used. Giving a *true* gift can be a wonderful experience for both the "giver" and the "receiver."

A common error that psychotherapists of various persuasions, including psychologists and psychiatrists, make is that they tend to make *"sweeping generalizations"* without any real evidence to back up their statements. For example, a dear friend of mine, who happens to be a psychotherapist, was once told by her psychiatrist supervisor that the reason she never became a "doctor" was because she was "self-defeating." Knowing almost nothing about the life history and background of my friend, to make such a sweeping generalization was entirely unwarranted and very *grandiose*. In fact, I have found that the most pompous professionals practicing in the field of psychotherapy tend to make the most grandiose statements. No matter what type of credentials these people possess, a perspective client would do well to stay *far away* from them.

It is a basic principle in the practice of psychotherapy that the therapist must be able to clearly and objectively view his client. In order to do this, the therapist must know himself very well indeed. He does not want to impose his hang-ups on the client. This is a primary reason why *all* therapists, if they are to be maximally effective, need to be in therapy themselves, and basically complete it, before they practice it themselves.

In this age of psychology and psychiatry, it is very common for individuals to attribute physical symptoms to stress, anxiety, and any of a number of emotional causes. Chronic headaches, stomach distress, and the like are easily dismissed to some temporary emotional disturbance. In reality, this attitude can have serious, and even *dangerous* consequences. One must *always* assume that if an individual has physical symptoms that there is a biological basis for the condition. A medical evaluation is paramount. If the findings are negative, then, and only then can the person and the therapist feel confident that this is an emotionally based condition. There have been cases where people who were suffering from physical symptoms had gone only for individual psychotherapy, causing a biologically based condition to get significantly worse. In a few instances, people have actually *died*. (I.E. – patient being treated in therapy for chronic headaches, who dies subsequently of a brain tumor.)

It sometimes will happen that when an individual is trying to explain something to another person, that the latter may become upset. A good technique to employ at this point is to ask the person, "What did you hear me just say to you?" I have seen in a number of instances where the individual will proceed to state something which is not at all what the other person had originally said, or is a partial distortion. This type of procedure can effectively "nip in the bud" a potentially unpleasant situation.

If you are having a conversation with another person, and are trying to determine how the other person is reacting, look at the individual's *eyes, mouth,* and *body posture.* A lot of valuable information can be obtained in this manner.

The period from two to four years of age in a child's life is particularly important if the child is going to develop some degree of *frustration tolerance.* During this period in the child's life, the parents must be firm and consistent in dealing with this issue in their child's life. If they are not, the child has an excellent chance of having behavioral problems as he grows older. In this world, all of us have to wait for things. The parents must work on instilling some sense of this during this age period.

In the academic development of our children, the early elementary years are probably the most crucial in developing a true interest, and "love of learning." As such, our highest paid, and most skilled teachers, academically, emotionally, and socially should be found teaching the early elementary grades. While some teachers do function at this level (without the pay) many do not. This is why a number of children have been emotionally and educationally scarred by having a very poor teacher early in life. This situation needs to be corrected.

The period during and immediately after the birth of a child will have both great rewards and great stresses. If handled properly, the marriage can become even stronger, or, on the other hand, it can be significantly damaged. For example, some husbands during this period will try to be "extra tuned in" to their wives, being a big asset to both her and the new baby. On the other hand, some husbands will bemoan the extra burden of having a baby and expect their wives to make it up to them. This latter attitude and behavior will typically anger and even enrage his wife, and may cause a significant rift in the relationship. Similarly, some husbands will understand the constant stresses in raising a young infant and child, and will try to encourage his wife to get out and relax when reasonable. Others will complain that their wife is simply "not the same woman anymore," expecting her to be exuberant and energetic at the end of a day of coping with a child or two or more children. I have noticed in a number of troubled marriages where the couples came for therapy, that this period in their lives was often a major factor in causing dissension within the marriage.

It is one of the great pleasures in life to be able to occasionally just "hang out," and do nothing. The ability to do this is part of being "nice" to oneself. It is also a sign of having some degree of "inner peace." It is a pity that so many of us really cannot "relax." It can also be a sign that these people have "lost touch" with themselves.

It is very helpful in a relationship to be able to determine whether your mate tends to overdramatize their feelings and what transpired in situations; tends to understate their feelings and what happened in situations; or tends to realistically convey how he is feeling, and to accurately describe what occurred in a given situation. For example, if your mate is prone to exaggeration, when he is *very* upset, this might translate into being *mildly* upset. Similarly, if your mate tends to understate things, and says that he is mildly upset, this might well translate into "I am *very* upset." Of course, *no* translation is required for the realistic conveyor of his feelings and of occurrences. An accurate appraisal of which category your mate falls into, can be *quite* helpful in dealing with them.

It is a sad commentary how popular such new devices as video games and cassette headphones are, for they are additional ways in which people can *avoid* relating to other human beings. It is quite sad to observe adolescents, adults, and even children spending hours playing these video games, often alone, or to observe individuals walking down the street, oblivious to those around them, as they are totally engrossed in the music reverberating in their head. These people are missing out on a much greater pleasure, a chance to get to know, and care about others, and have them care about you.

One major characteristic of emotionally mature individuals is that if they so desire, they can express their feelings, fantasies, and/or thoughts through the vehicle of *language*. On the other hand, emotionally immature individuals typically do *not* use language for expressing their feelings, fantasies, and/or thoughts, either because they are not consciously aware of them, or because they do not feel comfortable talking about them (probably because key people during their early years did not do so either). As a result, emotionally immature people tend to "act out" their "inner world" through behavior. For example, if an emotionally mature person is angry at another person's behavior, he most likely is aware of feeling this, and will tell the other person through talking in a constructive manner. On the other hand, the emotionally immature individual will tend to do something hostile toward the other person, or avoid them altogether, rejecting them in the process. The "acting out" of his angry feelings does nothing constructive, it just damages the relationship. If the latter individual goes for psychotherapy, one sign of significant progress will be when he is using language more to express his/her feelings, fantasies, and/or thoughts, relying on using unproductive, and even anti-social behavior less and less.

As amazing as it may seem neither clinical psychologists, nor psychiatrists, nor certified social workers have to be analyzed before they can practice psychotherapy on another human being.

Many people talk about how they would "love" to have a special relationship. Yet when you observe some of these same people actually relating to another person, you may well hear and see things done which are insensitive and may even be mean, indicating just the opposite. Perhaps the most disheartening aspect of this, is that these people are very often really *unaware* about what their words and actions are conveying to someone else. For example, some men talk about dating "chicks," and "foxes," not even giving women human status. With such an attitude, their chances of having a mature, loving relationship are practically nil.

It is not uncommon to see a couple arguing in front of friends or relatives. This is insensitive, as well as unproductive. It is humiliating to both individuals, embarrassing to the other people, and suggests a lack of respect for each other, and for the relationship. If something bothers an individual about his mate's behavior while in public, it is wise to wait to discuss the matter in the privacy of one's home, or if you are so upset that you cannot wait, then ask your mate to go off to a private area, excusing oneself from the group temporarily.

The minority of individuals who commit terrible crimes *are* severely mentally ill, and were out of touch with reality at the time of their crime or crimes. These psychotic individuals are *not* responsible for themselves, and their actions. They should be placed in mental hospitals for appropriate treatment for their psychotic illness.

Many people believe that individuals who kill others, or commit other types of heinous crimes must be "mentally ill." In fact, it appears that the majority of these felons, rather than being severely mentally ill, and out of touch with reality (psychotic), *are* actually aware of their environment, and rules of society. They choose to callously break these rules. As such these *sociopaths* basically suffer from a lack of moral development, and thus have a lack of *conscience*. It is my opinion that these people be held fully responsible for their actions, and be dealt with accordingly.

There are individuals in our society who believe that if they say they are sorry, or cry, that they *must* automatically be forgiven by the individual they have offended. Depending on what they have said or done, an apology is sometimes *not* sufficient. These same individuals do not understand typically, that even if the other person does accept this person's apology, it may *take time* for the former to again feel as warm to this person.

Some people live their lives on the basis of "should's," and "ought to's," as opposed to listening to their feelings and needs. As a result, they will tend to miss out on being spontaneous, as well as cutting down on the enjoyment and satisfaction that life can offer.

Some people are forever spending their lives complaining over why is my life the way it is, and why isn't it the way I want. They use enormous quantities of energy in this endeavor. They do not understand that life deals each of us a hand each day, and it is our responsibility to *cope* with this "hand" as best we can. The former position is both unrealistic, as well as self-centered.

The more emotionally mature an individual is, the more he is aware that each person has *many* facets to his personality. The emotionally mature individual does not focus on a single detail, and then proceed to stereotype the person as being worthwhile and desirable, or worthless and undesirable. Instead he will tend to eagerly try to know as many aspects of the other person's personality in an endeavor to really get to know this person. As a result, if you ask an emotionally healthy individual to describe a friend, he can present a fairly comprehensive picture, with all sorts of hues and nuances. On the other hand, an emotionally immature person, when asked the same thing, has little to offer, relying on cliches and platitudes.

One of the major indicators that a person has completed his therapy, is when the client can now look at his parents as being *human beings*, complete with strengths, liabilities, anxieties and fears. This is a *wonderful* accomplishment.

In our raising of children, we can emotionally injure them through both acts of *commission* and acts of *omission*. For example, I have heard clients complain bitterly how their mother did this to them, and that to them, giving a number of abusive acts over the years. When asked about their *father's* role, they would initially comment how nice he was to the client. In some cases, however, it subsequently became apparent that the father emotionally wounded his child by *not being there* when the child typically needed him (this probably putting more pressure on the mother, contributing to more abusive behavior on her part). This lack of nurturance and guidance by the child's father resulted in certain emotional difficulties which were not obvious to the client because they were caused by acts of *omission*. In essence, both of these types of actions can have deleterious effects on the child's emotional and social development.

It is rare in families for one family member to be a total ogre, and the other parent to be a "saint." Emotionally immature individuals often have a need to view one parent as being simply wonderful, if the other is particularly abusive. I have seen in a number of instances, where one parent was openly hostile and/or rejecting to a child, while the "saintly" parent was actually implicitly or *covertly* hostile and/or rejecting to this same child, but the latter cannot or will not see this as such. For example, I once heard a friend describe having a very cruel father, who would periodically throw him out of the house. In trying to illustrate how wonderful his mother was, he proudly proclaimed that she always threw his coat out to him so he would not be cold (there being no conscious awareness of the mother not protecting and defending her son, but rather simply giving *approval* to this cruel behavior by throwing out the person's coat).

In raising children, it is important that both parents present a *"united front"* when it comes to discipline or family rules. If a parent disagrees with the way the other parent is handling the child, they should talk to their mate *in private*. This shows respect for one's mate, and this type of unified stance by both parents will prevent the child from learning to manipulate one parent against the other, which would hinder the child's development.

Emotionally mature individuals try to be simply *themselves*, irrespective of who they are with, or the particular circumstances at the moment. On the other hand, emotionally immature people may try to tailor their personalities to get others to approve and like them. This "chameleon-type" behavior indicates an intrinsic lack of faith in oneself, and suggests a poor self-image.

If an individual is being interviewed for a big job, or is out on an important date, he may question how to act. In reality, this person should simply be himself. If the person tries to be someone or something he is not, and the situation does *not* work out, they will always wonder, "What would have happened if I had just been me?" If it does work out, the person may well feel compelled to continue to "act" for fear of exposing one's true self. On the other hand, the person who is himself in all situations, has the comfort, irrespective of the result, that he was just the way he really is. This indicates a liking for oneself and a self-respect.

Sexual chemistry is one of the easiest things to understand: if it is present, then it is present; if it is not present, then it is not. It is sad how many people cannot accept this, and waste vast quantities of energy and time, trying to force another person to feel what is not there.

When parents speak to their young children, they need to pay particular attention to the level of *vocabulary* they use. I have heard fathers say, for example, to their three year old daughters, "Darling, are you feeling perturbed?" Using words that are age-appropriate will greatly help the communication between parent and child.

In general, parents need to avoid getting into "long-winded" explanations when talking to their children. Why is this? This is because their children will tend to quickly lose interest in what is being said and, as a result, will tend to "tune-out" what his parent is saying.

It is important that a parent realize when his child is "really starting to get to him." In these instances, it is wise to send the child to his room, until both the parent and the child are calmer, so as to prevent the parent from physically and/or emotionally abusing the child.

I have met a number of individuals in and out of therapy, who pride themselves as being emotionally independent of their parents. They state they are in *no* way dependent on their parents; if the latter recommend a given course of action, they will *never* follow this advice. If mama or papa say do "A," this type of person will immediately do "B." If mama or papa like a given individual, these same people will tend to begin disliking this person. In reality, these people are *not at all* emotionally independent of their parents; they are actually *pseudo-independent*, very much influenced by what their parents say and do. A truly emotionally independent individual listens carefully to what his parents state, weigh it carefully, and then either go along with what is recommended or not go along with it, depending on their inner values and belief system. To simply reject what your family suggests because it is coming from them is really a sign of being *very* attached to them, and indeed is giving them *a lot of power* over the person's life.

There are many known reasons for a child being hyperactive (overactive). Diet, minimal brain dysfunction, physical illness, boredom, and emotional difficulties are some of the more common causes. However, many parents are not aware that there is a relationship between the child's level of language development and degree of hyperactivity. The less adept a child is in using language to communicate his needs, the greater the tendency to use movement or body activity to lessen tensions, and express inner desires and needs. As the child's command of language subsequently improves, the hyperactivity related to its former inefficiency should also decrease.

Many people, clients and therapists are very involved with studying dreams. There have been all kinds of theories advanced to what psychological function or functions are served by dreaming. In my opinion, dreams represent an individual's attempt to work out something that he is not at peace with from the past, present, or both, while the person is sleeping. In my opinion, therapists often *misuse* dream analysis in two primary ways; they make the dream almost the *entire focus* of the therapy, ignoring the *relationship* between therapist and client, and/or they have a cookbook approach to dream analysis, where a given image in the dream has to have a *universal* meaning (i.e. − a stick *must* symbolically represent a penis). In actuality, each dream, and every element within it, is a *highly personalized* experience for a given individual, and must be investigated and respected as such for dream analysis to be of any significant value in the emotional development of the client.

It has baffled me for a long time why anyone would pay the astronomical fees of psychiatrists (i.e. − $85 − $100 for a typical 45 minute session), unless they require medication. Since the vast majority of therapy clients do *not* require such an intervention, why would they pay such large sums for a medical school training, which has *little or nothing* to do with the actual practice of psychotherapy. I doubt that these same clients would pay extra money for a musician who studied a number of years to attain a doctorate in foreign languages.

Some individuals are quick to "blame" a child's parents for any or all maladies that the child suffers from. This is both unfair, and insensitive. For example, the childhood psychosis called "early infantile autism" illustrates this point nicely. For years parents of these children were lambasted for being "cold," "aloof," and "rejecting" causing their children to develop the over-and-under reactivity to sensory stimuli, the erratic developmental rate, the severe interpersonal problems, and the severe language difficulties associated with this disorder. In fact, some professionals still are "blaming" the parents of these children, when there is increasing evidence that this disorder is due to some sort of *brain dysfunction*.

Although licensed clinical psychologists, and certified social workers are legally not allowed to prescribe or administer medication, it is their responsibility to know certain things about these medications if they plan on doing competent therapy. Specifically, they should know when to send a client to a medical doctor for medicine (the symptoms that warrant it), the basic categories of drugs; how they work, as well as possible side-effects. There are a number of professionals in these two disciplines who know nothing about medication, and as a result, their clients may sometimes suffer considerable psychic pain and physical discomfort because of this type of professional ignorance (i.e. − as in the case of moderate or serious depression).

When people come for marriage therapy, they typically want the psychologist to "fix our marriage." In actuality, a psychologist cannot offer any *guarantees*. He can only help the couple understand clearly the problems that exist in the marriage; explore ways of trying to eliminate these difficulties; and then help each person decide whether he is willing and able to make the necessary adjustments, and still feel enhanced and satisfied by the "new" relationship. Many people do *not* understand that after these steps occur, that if the couple then decides to "breakup," that the marriage therapy may still be considered to be a "success." Why is this? This is because there are couples who are so unhappy, but out of fear and dependency stay together. If, after ending the marriage, both people eventually find greater inner peace and happiness, then the marriage therapy was indeed "a success."

The *milder* forms of emotional disturbance (neurosis) appear to be largely the result of adverse *environmental* factors, while the more *severe* forms of mental illness (psychosis) tend to involve a significant biological basis as well.

It is important that, as parents, we *respect* our children's fears, and not try to deny, or ridicule them for having these fears. All children will experience *normal* developmental fears as they pass through childhood, and what they most need from their parents is *understanding, emotional support,* and *gentle reassurances.* Too many times, parents try to be very logical in explaining that this object or event is not a fearful one in and of itself, neglecting to focus on the child's fearful response. To deny or "put down" the child's feeling is to alienate that child from his parents (i.e. – "You're afraid of this clown? That's ridiculous. A clown never hurts a child. He likes kids," as opposed to "You're feeling afraid of the clown? What can I do to help you feel better?" with a discussion of clowns occurring later on).

It is all too common for an individual to alienate and/or anger his mate, by making *plans* without first discussing them with the latter. This presumptuousness indicates an insensitivity to the rights and feelings of your partner, and does nothing to endear oneself to the other person. It is caring and respectful to talk things over before making definitive plans for both oneself and one's partner.

Many married couples believe that the only alternative they have is a divorce, if the two people are not getting along, and conventional marriage therapy is not proving to be effective. In actuality, a viable option is what I like to call a "controlled trial separation," where the two individuals live apart from one another; where each person sees the same psychologist for individual therapy once a week, and every two to four weeks both parties come for a session together with the psychologist. This "controlled trial separation" arrangement enables each person to try out new lifestyles, independently of their mate, and at the same time utilize the individual sessions for looking at oneself, the marriage, and one's life, in general. The occasional group sessions enable the couple, with the psychologist's assistance, to keep "in touch" under controlled conditions, and access what each is learning, and ascertain whether the two people want to eventually reconcile, and if so, what has to be done to make this a reality. I have found this to be a very effective procedure.

Many adopted individuals have poor self-images, related to having not been wanted by their biological parents. What they refuse to look at, sometimes, is how they are indeed, *special*. Unlike children who are being raised by their biological parents, adopted children can be *sure* their *new* parents really wanted them, since they went through a *great* deal to adopt this child. When they *emotionally* can accept this, their self-image should improve.

Emotionally mature people view authority figures, first and foremost as *human beings*. As such, they are aware that these authority figures, such as doctors, will have all levels of competency reflected within their profession ranging from totally incompetent to superbly competent. In contrast, emotionally immature individuals tend to make professionals "God" or view all of them as being incompetent. In addition, emotionally mature individuals take responsibility for their lives, and while they respect the recommendations of the authority figure, such as a medical doctor, they view the latter as a consultant and, as such, will make the final decision for themselves. This is in contrast to the emotionally immature person, who may place the entire responsibility for their lives in the hands of the authority figure.

While the telephone is indeed a wonderful invention, and is many times the only available option to relate directly to another human being, it can also cause real difficulties if not properly utilized. I have witnessed several cases, where great damage to a relationship has been due to an "ugly" argument over the telephone. Given many nonverbal cues (i.e. — facial expressions, eye contact, posture) are eliminated by phone conversations, this significantly enhances the chance of *misunderstandings* occurring while relating over the telephone. Therefore, individuals should try to have "deep" conversations *in person*, not over the telephone, if possible, and should try to keep most conversations by phone to a minimal length. This philosophy could have helped many a relationship and many a phone bill!

Some couples believe that they must do "everything" together. Even if one member really does not want to go to the movies, he must either go, or his wife cannot go alone. Similarly, if he wants to go dancing and she does not really want to, they will either both go, or neither will go. In essence, this is really a "smothering" and "controlling" stance, which suggests an underlying insecurity in one or both individuals, and a lack of trust in the relationship. In an emotionally mature relationship, if one person wants to go swimming, and the other is too tired or not "in the mood," it is perfectly acceptable for the other to go swim, and for the latter to stay home, and "take it easy." At the basis of such behavior is a freedom, mutual respect and trust (of course, I am *not* talking about couples constantly going their separate ways, suggesting they do not want to be together).

When a couple divorce, they are divorcing *each other*, not their *children*. I have seen an increasing number of cases where one member of the marriage acts as if now that I am divorced I have *no further responsibilities*, except perhaps financial to my children. This is an unfair, insensitive, and yes, even cruel attitude, since the children are helpless victims, who deserve even *more* sensitivity and loving actions on the part of both parents given the additional stresses and pressures they will have to cope with.

It is fairly common in our society to meet someone who is already involved with another person, or may be in the process of terminating a relationship. Too many times, the latter may inadvertently or on purpose try to draw you into what is happening in the other relationship. In these instances, it is important to not allow the other person to place his or her "emotional burdens" on to you, as this is really *"none of your business."* The other individual should either continue to see this other person, or indeed terminate the relationship, but in either case, you do not need to hear, and do not need to deal with it at all. Too many of us get entangled in these types of situations, causing needless anguish and unhappiness.

Some individuals, in and out of therapy, are very concerned with the question, "Do most parents really love their children?" In my opinion, most parents *do*, indeed, love their children. However, many of these parents do *not* know how to *show* their love through *loving actions* and *words*. Why is this? This is mainly due to *ignorance*, and because they themselves were not shown how to act lovingly by their parents (your grandparents). It is certainly difficult to act a certain way, if we have not observed such behavior when we were growing up.

Some individuals can almost never enjoy an activity because they are *so* afraid of having it taken away from them. Similarly, if these individuals are feeling happy, they are fearful of losing this feeling. In some sense, they are their *own worst enemy*. They are constantly on the "alert," looking out for misfortune. It is a sad waste of time and energy.

A major cause of disenchantment and dissension in a relationship is due to *"double standards."* Namely, if the husband goes out weekly with the "boys," then his wife should have the same option to go out with her friends. Similarly, if the husband has been bringing home the only source of revenue over the years, and this has been family money, then if the wife subsequently gets a job also, she cannot, in fairness, decide that the money she earns is hers. I have seen this type of "double standard" behavior in a number of troubled relationships. In essence, for a relationship to work out, there must be fairness and parity, perhaps above all, where both individuals are given equal options, and work as a "team," rather than in selfish, self-serving ways.

One of the most interesting observations I have noted concerning people, is that there is sometimes *little* correlation between how attractive, how intelligent, or how nice a given person is, and how much they value and care about themselves. Why is this? This is because the way we feel about ourselves is primarily due to the *input* (both words and actions) that we experienced from our family members as we were growing up.

Some people are forever arriving late for appointments, forgetting to fulfill promises to others, managing to only partially complete a task for another, and the like. These same people may actually view themselves as nice, caring human beings. In reality, they are exhibiting passive-aggressive behaviors, which reflect insensitivity, callousness, and hostility on a covert level.

It is not an uncommon occurrence for individuals who go for therapy to periodically bitterly criticize one or both of their parents for having done this to the person, or that to the person. While it certainly can be helpful for the therapy client, and even his parent or parents to sit down and talk things out, it is *not* acceptable behavior to attack one's parents on a personal level. Too many times, guilt-ridden parents absorb all kinds of verbal abuse from their children who are in therapy. To do so is *not* beneficial to either the parent or parents or to their child. Verbal or behavioral "attacks" will only cause increased "hard" feelings, and alienation. On the other hand, telling a parent how one feels about certain occurrences in a respectful manner *is* constructive.

Sometimes, clients in the midst of their therapy keep "throwing up to their parents" particular incidents in the child's life. Related statements about the same episodes is typically *not* productive; it only engenders guilt in one's parents, generally. A parent can only apologize, and explain one's past behavior, and try to relate better to his child in the *present*. Remember, an individual *cannot go back* and undo the past, but can only *learn* from it.

It is ironic that admission to clinical psychology programs, as well as medical school, is largely based on marks, graduate record examination scores, or MCAT scores, and the like. While these indices reflect intellectual functioning, they do *not* measure sensitivity, perceptiveness, warmth, emotional health, and relating skills, the *hallmarks of a good clinician*.

In trying to help your child develop a good self-image, it is extremely important that parents pay close attention to the *tone* in their voices when they talk to them. More damage can sometimes be done to the child's self-image from a persistent hostile or disgusted tone, than by the actual words being said by his parents. If the parents are angry or otherwise upset about something which has nothing to do with the child, and their tone reflects this emotional state, it is wise for the parent to explain explicitly how he is feeling, and that the child is not the problem at all. This discrimination is important in helping to maintain the child's good self-image.

There will come a time in this society when no woman would either call herself, or allow herself to be called, "Mrs. John Doe," or "Mrs. Harry Smith." There will also come a time where no woman will give up her maiden name to assume her husband's last name. This will occur when women want to be equal partners with their future husbands, with neither party "taking care" of the other, in a parent-child sense. When this transpires, it will be better for women, for men, and for their relationships.

Some clinical psychologists and psychiatrists seem to "love" to speak in technical language. There may be a number of plausible explanations for this type of behavior. For example, some professionals like to "hide" behind psychological or psychiatric terminology to create an aura, where their clients cannot "challenge" the psychologist or psychiatrist because the latter simply does not understand what is being said. Also, occasionally, a professional will try to hide his humanness or even incompetence behind a sea of technical language. In essence, it is my opinion, that a competent, emotionally healthy psychologist or psychiatrist should be able to explain *any* technical term in simple language that can be comprehended by any individual of average intelligence.

Some people spend a good part of their life planning to retire. On the other hand, emotionally mature individuals do not look forward to simply "hanging out." Instead, they tend to view their lives as having a number of "chapters," and when one chapter is completed they will go on to write another, facing new challenges along the way. This latter viewpoint is shown by the increasing number of individuals who are planning second careers to pursue as they approach later life, and by the increasing number of "senior citizens" who are now attending colleges across the country in an endeavor to *enrich* their lives.

I sometimes think that the fields of psychology and psychiatry would be better off if they tended *not* to label (diagnose) so-called "mental disorders," aside from perhaps using a very general label such as "psychosis" or "neurosis" to indicate if an individual is or is not "in touch" with reality. I have witnessed case conferences where five different professionals may have studied a client, and come up with three, four, or *even* five very different diagnoses. This is truly a sad commentary.

Many people believe that an individual who goes for psychotherapy must be "crazy." In reality, most individuals who go for psychotherapy do so simply because they are "unhappy," either with themselves, with their lives, or both. Indeed, it indicates some degree of *emotional health* for a person to look at himself and say I can use some professional help for my problems. Often, the people who require individual psychotherapy the *most*, are the *very* individuals who would be *least* prone to go.

Some people literally cannot bear to have mixed feelings (ambivalence) about anything. They want to feel *either* one way *or* another. Unfortunately, such ambivalence is a major part of life.

It is not uncommon when a person tells others that he is thinking of going for psychotherapy, or has actually just begun going, that his friends, and/or family will put pressure on the person not to go, stating that there is nothing wrong with this person. This is an *uncaring*, and *selfish* position. These people are not really responding and respecting the individual's feelings and needs; rather, they are responding out of their own *fears, guilt* and *ignorance.*

The more emotionally and socially aware an individual is, the more he is aware how easy it is for any of us to attribute motivations for a given person's behavior based largely or even entirely on *conjecture.* Therefore, whenever another person acts in a certain way, or says something that can be taken in more than one way, the emotionally mature individual will immediately ask how this was meant. This technique can help prevent the build up of misunderstandings and hidden animosities.

When an individual finds a loving person to relate to, this can be a type of "therapy," in the sense that one's self-image can be improved from this experience. It will largely depend on whether the former will let this new person get emotionally close, or keep the person at a distance.

Some people believe that it is absolutely "horrible" that sex education is being taught in schools. On the contrary, since many parents do not provide their children with adequate, or in fact, any sex education, it is imperative that schools therefore provide *accurate* information. If sex education is presented within the *total* context of a child or adolescent's emotional and social development, and takes into account the age, and level of understanding of the individuals then it can have an extremely beneficial and positive affect. In essence, what is wrong with knowing more about *ourselves*, given the responsibilities involved are clearly stated?

Isn't it the height of arrogance for an individual to try to dictate what two consenting adults do in the privacy of their bedroom? This type of person should concentrate on his sexual behavior, and not try to control others. With all the pressing problems that exist in this society, surely the latter requires our attention much more than what two people are doing sexually to enjoy themselves and each other.

When two individuals state that they are in "love" with one another, it might be beneficial to ask each other, "Exactly what does that mean that you say you love me." Why is this? Many people mean *many different* things when they say, "I love you," and a brief discussion at the outset might save a lot of pain and emotional grief.

104

Did you ever listen to someone discuss an emotional reaction in a given situation, which you, yourself have experienced. In general, did you notice the feelings of closeness and humanness you felt when this happened?

Sometimes two individuals do all the "right things;" they talk out their differences in a respectful manner; they go for professional counseling or psychotherapy if this does not work, etc. If they still cannot work out their differences, the only thing they can do is separate for a while, and see if *time*, and their new life experiences will change their attitudes and feelings for one another in a positive direction.

If reasonable, it can be a wonderful thing to get your child a pet such as a dog, cat, etc. This can help teach the child about caring and being responsible for a living being. Also, the "unconditional love" that a child can get from a loving animal can be of significant benefit in the child developing a good self-image. However, the child must be old enough to be able to understand what he can and cannot do to this animal, since both the child and the pet may suffer if the child does not understand the responsibilities and limitations involved.

Some people believe that if they are, or have been in psycho-therapy that they are now "polished professionals" ready to analyze anyone and everyone. This is absolutely untrue.

When an individual invests a lot of energy in not allowing his feelings to be expressed (such as anger), this can rob the individual of spontaneity, as well as causing a generalized emotional constriction of the person's personality. I have seen a number of such individuals in therapy, who came in presenting a timid, withdrawn, extremely soft-spoken exterior. As these people began to feel that they had basic "rights" in relating to others, and were not "bad" to have certain feelings such as anger, and also learned how to constructively express their feelings, a wonderful change occurred in each of them. A new vitality began to emerge; they began to exhibit a whole new range of emotions, and they all became much more spontaneous. In essence, these people had become much more "human" and "alive."

Sometimes, when a therapy client is behaving selfishly, callously and/or even hostilely toward the psychologist, and refuses to look at this behavior pattern, it is best for the psychologist to end the therapy relationship. Interestingly, when this is done, the client may subsequently call to enter the therapy once again with a much more mature and motivated attitude. Why? This is because the psychologist may have been the first key person in the client's life who ever set "limits" with this person. This may be "down deep," exactly what this person has been looking for.

It is ironic, that the more a psychologist learns about people, about emotional problems, and various types of mental disorder, the more he realizes that there are questions to be answered, and things to learn.

Whenever I listen to someone present a new theory on how to treat people's emotional and social problems, I always focus mainly on how this person relates to me and the rest of the people present. If this person really has found the "best way" of doing therapy with people's problems, I would think it would reflect in his *own* relating skills. Too often, I have seen such individuals exhibit inadequate or even poor relating skills in these situations.

It is one of the great joys and satisfactions in life to help another human being become a *happy, productive* person.